DATE DUE			

1092

591.52   Sanders, John (John
SAN   Michael)

All about animal
migration.

700030   01379C

The Question & Answer Book

ALL ABOUT ANIMAL MIGRATIONS

ALL ABOUT ANIMAL MIGRATIONS

By John Sanders
Illustrated by Ray Burns

Troll Associates

Library of Congress Cataloging in Publication Data

Sanders, John (John Michael)
    All about animal migrations.

    (Question and answer book)
    Summary: Uses a question and answer format to present
basic information about animal migrations, such as why
animals migrate, how they know where they are going,
and which animal makes the longest migration.
    1. Animal migration—Miscellanea—Juvenile literature.
[1. Animals—Migration. 2. Questions and answers]
I. Burns, Raymond, 1924-   ill. II. Title. III. Se-
ries: Question and answer book.
QL754.S26   1984   591.52′5   83-6630
ISBN 0-89375-977-5
ISBN 0-89375-978-3 (pbk.)

Printed in the United States of America
10   9   8   7   6   5   4   3   2   1

What is migration?

Summer is over, and the cool, crisp days are growing shorter. Suddenly, the autumn silence is shattered by the sound of noisy honking. A flock of geese is passing high overhead, heading south to warmer lands for the winter.

When large numbers of animals travel from one place to another, we say they are *migrating*. The trip they take is called a *migration*. Many animals leave their homes and migrate to other places at certain times of the year. For some, the migration is a very long journey. For others, it may be very short.

What kinds of migrations are there?

Some animals make one-way migrations. Others make round trips, returning to their first home after a certain amount of time. Still others migrate, then bring their young into the world, and die. Later, their offspring make the return trip alone.

What sorts of animals migrate?

Animals of many different kinds make migrations. Toads hop from gardens to ponds. Robins fly from north to south. Salmon leave their ocean homes and swim to freshwater streams. Great clouds of butterflies head for special places at certain times of the year.

Why do animals migrate?

Why don't animals just stay in one place instead of moving to a new area? Scientists who study animal behavior have discovered many different reasons why animals migrate. Some move to get away from cold weather. Some travel to mate and give birth. Others migrate to find food. Some even migrate to keep their homes from becoming too crowded.

How do animals know when to migrate?

People can look at calendars and clocks. But how do animals know when it is time to begin their migrations?

Scientists think that the length of the day may be the "calendar" for some animals. A decrease or increase in daylight hours may be the signal to be on the move. For others, changes in temperature may be a signal.

How do animals know where they are going?

Migrating birds can watch for familiar landmarks, such as rivers or coastlines, on their journeys. They may also use the sun and the stars to guide them. But what about other animals? Do they have built-in calendars, clocks, and compasses? We don't know. We do know that migration is a strange and mysterious fact of life for many animals, including certain birds, insects, fish, amphibians, reptiles, and mammals.

Where do butterflies go?

Some migrations are easy to recognize. In early fall, you might see long, fluttering lines of Monarch butterflies heading south. Some of them will fly nearly 2,000 miles (3,200 kilometers). They spend the winter in such places as California and along the Gulf of Mexico.

The butterflies settle down on tree branches and shrubs, half asleep. So many Monarchs cluster together that they seem to form colorful blossoms on "butterfly trees." Scientists have counted more than a hundred butterflies on a branch that is only 1 foot (30 centimeters) long!

In the spring, the Monarchs begin the return trip north. On the way, the female butterflies deposit their eggs and then die. When the eggs hatch, the new butterflies continue the northward migration. The next fall, they fly south, just as their parents did. They even return to the same trees!

9

Have you ever seen a ladybug's migration?

Some migrations are not so easy to recognize. If you ever watched a ladybug move from your garden to a warm crack in the garden wall, you may have been watching a migration. Other ladybugs may travel farther—they may fly to the mountains, where they spend the winter clustered together in large groups. In the spring, they return to their old homes.

Scientists are puzzled by these and many other migrations. How do the animals know where to go? How do they know when it is time to leave? No one knows all the answers.

Have you ever seen an "army of ants"?

The ants of the Amazon jungle in South America make periodic trips, but no one knows why. They aren't searching for food, because they often leave food behind. They don't seem to be heading for a particular place. But for some unknown reason, they become an army on the move.

As the army moves along, soldier ants attack and eat any living thing that happens to be in their path. Through thick forests and tangled jungles, the conquering ants march on.

11

When they come to a narrow river or stream, they may cross on a stalk or blade of grass that is long enough to reach the other side. Or they may build a bridge by running into the water and clinging to each other. Many are swept downstream, but there are so many ants in the army that they finally manage to build a "living bridge." Then the rest of the army marches over the bridge.

12

If the river is wide, the ants swarm into an "ant ball." The queen and the eggs are protected in the middle of the ball. The ball rolls into the water and drifts with the current. Ants on the bottom keep working their way to the top. Because of this constant movement, few of them drown. When the ball reaches the other side of the river, the ants break up, form their army again, and continue marching.

They may stop and stay in a rotten log or hollow tree while the queen lays up to 30,000 eggs. Then they move on, taking the eggs with them.

Why are they always on the move? Where are they going? We don't know. In fact, *they* may not even know where they are going. Perhaps they don't have any particular destination. It is a mystery yet to be solved.

Which animal makes the longest migration?

Many animal travelers head for a particular spot when they migrate. Some, like the Arctic tern, must travel a long, long way to get there. This bird is the champion long-distance traveler of the animal world.

How long is the migration of the Arctic tern?

Arctic terns travel so they can have summer weather all year round. In fact, their usual migration allows them to live in almost constant daylight. Every year, these slender black-and-white birds make a round trip of about 22,000 miles (35,200 kilometers). That's almost as far as a trip all the way around the world.

Arctic terns breed and nest in the far north during the summer season. Because the North Pole is tilted toward the sun at that time of year, the sun appears above the horizon almost all the time. These long daylight hours enable the terns to find and catch plenty of small ocean fish for themselves and their young.

Then, in late summer or early fall, as the days grow shorter and colder in the Arctic, the terns start their journey south. They travel all the way to Antarctica. Alaskan terns follow the Pacific coastlines of North and South America. Other terns fly from other northern nesting areas and meet near the British Isles. From there, they head south to the African coast, swooping down to catch fish from the Atlantic Ocean along the way.

Once in Africa, the flocks of terns split up. Some fly west toward Brazil, then south to Antarctica. The rest continue south to the Cape of Good Hope, then on to Antarctica. Later, they all return to their northern homes.

What tells Arctic terns when it is time to travel?

Perhaps it is a change in temperature, combined with a change in daylight hours. But no matter what the reasons, these animal travelers make their fantastic round-trip migration every year.

Which animals migrate to find food?

One of the reasons many animals migrate is to find the best food supply. Dolphins feed on schools of fish and squid. When their food supply swims north in spring, the dolphins follow. In the winter, they swim south again.

Great herds of Alaskan caribou roam the coastal plains of Alaska, eating mosses and grasses in spring and summer. Then, in early fall, they move south to the evergreen forests, where the food supply is better. A caribou may travel as much as 1,000 miles (1,600 kilometers) during its yearly migrations.

Which animals seek breeding grounds?

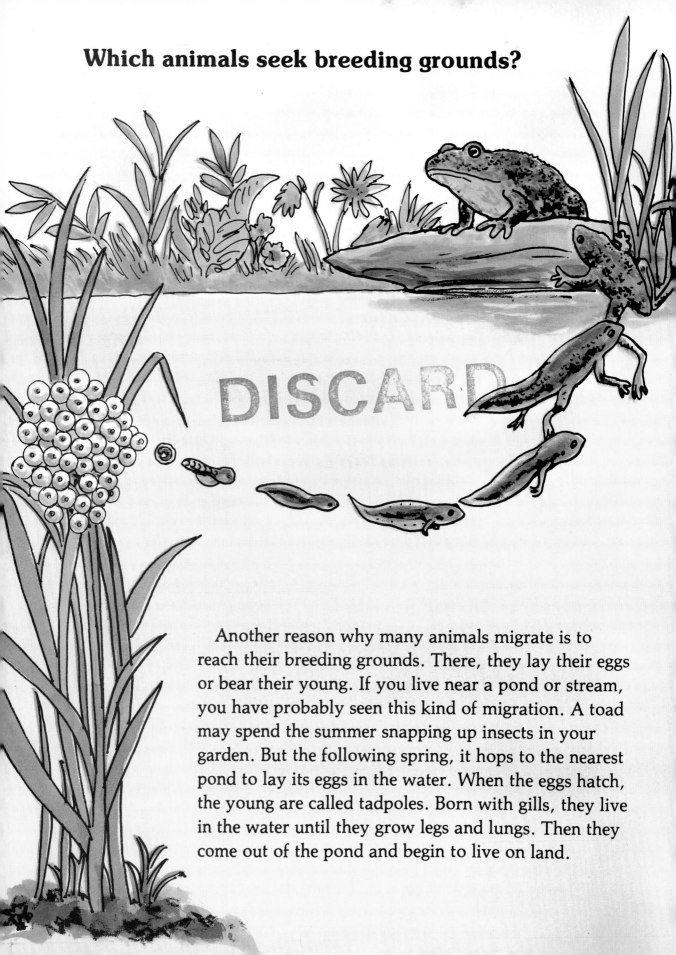

Another reason why many animals migrate is to reach their breeding grounds. There, they lay their eggs or bear their young. If you live near a pond or stream, you have probably seen this kind of migration. A toad may spend the summer snapping up insects in your garden. But the following spring, it hops to the nearest pond to lay its eggs in the water. When the eggs hatch, the young are called tadpoles. Born with gills, they live in the water until they grow legs and lungs. Then they come out of the pond and begin to live on land.

Alligators and crocodiles do just the opposite. They live most of their lives in the water. But when it is time to lay their eggs, the females move from the water of the river to the swampy shores. There, they build nests out of grass and weeds. Then they guard their eggs until they hatch.

Where do the sea turtles go?

Green sea turtles also lay their eggs on land. But they make a long migration to a particular place before they crawl out of the water.

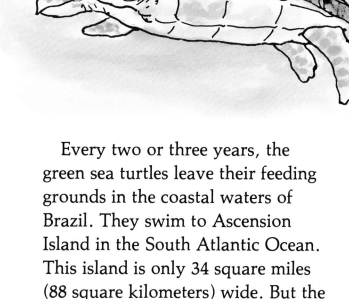

Every two or three years, the green sea turtles leave their feeding grounds in the coastal waters of Brazil. They swim to Ascension Island in the South Atlantic Ocean. This island is only 34 square miles (88 square kilometers) wide. But the turtles travel more than 1,000 miles (1,600 kilometers) to reach it.

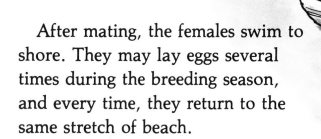

After mating, the females swim to shore. They may lay eggs several times during the breeding season, and every time, they return to the same stretch of beach.

When the eggs hatch, the young sea turtles begin their own migration. Even though they may not even be able to see the water, they always head in the direction of the sea. Many of them don't make it, for other hungry animals make meals of them. But some of the turtles do reach the sea. And they head for their parents' feeding grounds—even though they have never been there before.

When they are old enough, they will return to Ascension Island to lay their own eggs on the beaches. Why do they come to this lonely island? How do they find it? Scientists have not yet solved these riddles. They only know that the turtles seem to have some kind of "built-in compass."

Do seals migrate?

Yes. Northern fur seals make a very long migration each year. The females travel a round trip of about 6,000 miles (9,600 kilometers). From May until November, the seals reproduce on the Pribilof Islands, located off southwestern Alaska. Then both the males and females swim away from the islands. The males stay in the area of the Gulf of Alaska. But the females make a much longer trip. They swim south for 3,000 miles (4,800 kilometers). Their destination is southern California.

What sort of migration do whales make?

If you are ever near San Diego Bay in southern California during March or April, you can see another remarkable migration. It is the migration of the gray whales. These huge mammals make a round-trip migration of about 12,000 miles (19,200 kilometers) each year.

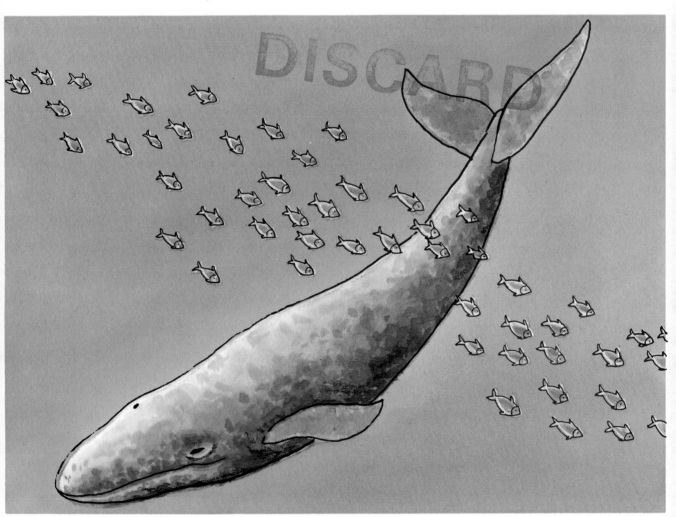

The gray whales spend the summer in the northern Pacific, feeding on small, shrimp-like sea animals called krill. Then, in early fall, they begin their migration, heading south to the quiet lagoons of southern California.

The pregnant females are the first to complete the journey. In December, they give birth to their calves, which are about 13 feet (4 meters) long. A month later, other females arrive and are joined by the males for the mating season.

In March, all the whales begin the return trip north to their summer feeding grounds. They pass San Diego about a mile (1.6 kilometers) off shore. People line the coast just to watch the spectacular sight as countless whales swim by.

24

How do scientists "track" migrations?

It wouldn't be hard to follow the path of the gray whales all the way to their destination in the northern Pacific. But tracking other migrating animals can be more difficult. One way to find out where animals go when they migrate is to tag or band them.

Wildlife experts often capture birds and fasten a coded band to each bird's leg. The code tells where each bird was originally banded. If a banded bird is found in another area at a later date, more about its travel habits is learned.

Other animals may be "tagged" instead of banded. A small tag is fastened to the animal's body. Tags and bands can help wildlife experts keep track of many animals that migrate. But there are still many questions about migration that are unanswered.

Which fish migrate?

For a long time, scientists have been studying the puzzling and complicated migrations of two kinds of fish—the freshwater eel and the Pacific salmon. They know where these fish go, but they still don't know what triggers the strong urge to migrate.

In the fall, North American and European eels migrate from freshwater rivers to the Sargasso Sea, which is south of the island of Bermuda in the Atlantic Ocean. Scientists believe the eels lay their eggs in seaweed and then die.

When the eggs hatch, the tiny new eels, called *larvae*, are each about the size of a fingernail. The babies begin to drift toward land. Young North American eels drift toward the United States and Canada. Their drifting migration takes about a year. Young European eels, spawned in a different part of the Sargasso Sea, drift toward Europe. Their journey is longer and will take from two to three years.

As they drift toward distant shores, the tiny larvae change to narrow, transparent creatures called *glass eels.* Then they grow larger and turn black. By the time they reach shore, they are called *elvers.* The male elvers stay near tidal marshes and saltwater harbors, while the females swim upstream.

Several years later, the eels will begin the same mysterious migration their parents once made—from freshwater rivers to the salty Sargasso Sea.

The migration of Pacific salmon is almost the opposite. After spending their lives in the salty sea, these fish swim as far as 2,000 miles (3,200 kilometers) to freshwater breeding streams. They must hurdle waterfalls and swim against powerful rapids to reach their breeding places.

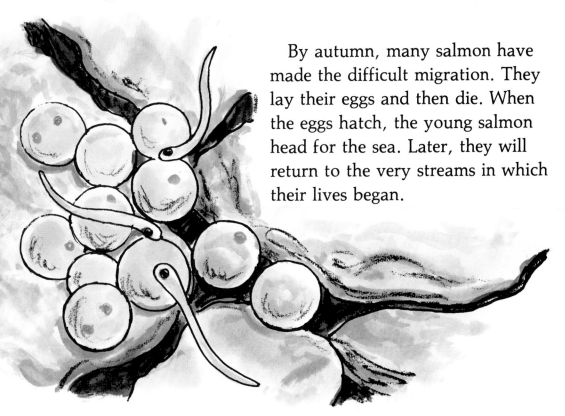

By autumn, many salmon have made the difficult migration. They lay their eggs and then die. When the eggs hatch, the young salmon head for the sea. Later, they will return to the very streams in which their lives began.

How does a salmon find its way back to its birthplace?

We don't know for sure. Scientists think they may use their sense of smell. But no matter how they do it, they are among the world's most famous animal travelers.

What famous animal travelers do you see?

Look around you. Robins may be flying south. Toads may be hopping from your garden to a pond. Tiny ladybugs may be moving toward their winter homes. Huge gray whales may be passing close to shore.

Why do they do it?

Animals migrate for food and for warmth. They migrate to breed and sometimes to die. Often they migrate for mysterious reasons that we do not completely understand. But every year, countless animals of all kinds repeat the journeys made by their ancestors.

Year after year, they migrate from one place to another. They are all part of a strange and fascinating world—the world of the animal travelers.